It Started When You Farted

Witty Rhymes For Playful Minds

By John Ormsby

&

Illustrated by Andrea Benko

Maple Syrup Publishing
ISBN: 978-1-7398674-1-6

Table of Contents

The critics ask from time to time:
Do all your poems have to rhyme?
If not the case, my esteemed friends
How would I know when each one ends?

J. Ormsby

Acknowledgements

This book would not have been possible without my family, friends, Andrea, Mo, Charris, Cher and St Jude.

For My Sister

(the funniest person I know)

Cat Nip

The difference between cats and dogs?
Hold each in an embrace
Your dog will share a loving nod
A cat will scratch your face

Creepy Crawler

A friend of mine who used to teach
Said some kids he just couldn't reach
A situation made more grim
For they were learning how to swim

Mist Opportunity

I’m known to stretch out on the lawn
Amidst the weekend carry on
Of mowing, trimming, watering
And folks I know I ought to ring

Just when it starts to get too loud
When life can push and kids can crowd
Before the next field’s needing ploughed
I lay right back and pick a cloud

The dogs, alerted, circle me
Unsure if they should stay or flee
They know each trick, each ruse I use
To wrestle them in ones and twos

Eventually they come to rest
On either side, heads on my chest
And then the three of us just stare
At our own clouds a way up there

Marshmallow Fluff or Dairy Whip
A giant dollop on the lip
Of Heaven, cruising like a ship
That's drifted, noiseless, from its slip

I want to jump and land on it
And try my best to stand on it
Then sink into its spongy core
While eating handfuls from its store

They have no map, no place to be
You can't catch clouds because they're free
To nonchalantly skirt your town
Then make you run when they come down

The trouble is, they take their time
And doing so, robs me of mine
So up I get – no time to lie!
Until the next cloud passes by...

Alcohol On You Later

My gran runs two teapots
(which tends to make her wee lots)
Her good one goes out on display
The other she keeps tucked away

When visitors decide to call
The posh pot serves them, one and all
Dispensing cups of Earl of Grey
From her brushed-silver serving tray

A person shouldn't trivialise
A ritual so civilised

When Elsie Burns who lives next door
Comes calling 'round each day at four
The Staffordshire is put away
For it's too late for Earl of Grey

Gran reaches for her other pot
Whose contents never need be hot
And pours her canny friend a cup
Of mother's homemade pick-me-up

A nip of whisky leaves them feeling
Life's too short to drink Darjeeling

Welcome To Finland

If killer whales stood on their tails
And walked out of the sea
A dog's next trick he'd learn real quick
Is how to climb a tree

Sleep Over

My love swears I snore like a bear
This is a husband's fate
A wife's is to give thankful prayer
That men don't hibernate

Creature Feature

When dining out we're well aware
Our manners are on view
We open doors like Fred Astaire
Insisting... *After you!*

Which silverware to use and when
And how to hold a glass
While tackling *pommes parisienne*
Delineate one's class

But not so in the cinema
The difference is stark
Because it's hard to be bourgeois
And crack nuts in the dark

The lighting's low so patrons know
When they're not being watched
It's fine to eat an Oreo
Retrieved from off your crotch

You eat out of a bucket
Like a con in county jail
And when you're done, you chuck it
Like a Molotov cocktail

Wonder what life's like inside
A real safari park?
Round up loads of humans
And then feed them in the dark

Consequential Confidential

I think at times, oh yes, I think
That I would make the best Rat Fink
The sort who listens to friends' tales
Then snitches, sending them to jails
For foolery and crimes and tricks
(those deeds which get you two-to-six)
But then again I'd better not
They are a vengeful, wicked lot
Who'd want to even up the score
For they know me and I've done more...

Job Done

A bear who needs to use The Gents
(one of life's everyday events)
Faces a pressing issue:
What does one use for tissue?
According to the local lore
Passed down by those who've gone before
Most bears will grab the nearest thing
To wipe away those bits that cling

A most hygienic habit
But tell that to the rabbit

Pointe Taken

Ballerinas stand on toes
To dazzle us with twirls
So, here's the question I would pose
Why not hire taller girls?

Against The Grain

Ever eaten whole grain bread
And sworn you'd chewed on bark instead?

Soup for One

I don't remember what I wore
Or who sat next to me
I don't remember who cried more
And who came just to see

I don't remember hymns they played
The readings that were read
Or why he paused before he said
That you weren't really dead

I just remember how you looked
When you slept next to me
The Sunday dinners that you cooked
And how you sipped your tea

Those corny jokes you always told
Which rarely made me laugh
How next to you I looked so old
In every photograph

I don't remember telling you
To leave me all alone

I don't remember telling you
I'd be fine on my own

I don't remember

Meal Deal

The female spider dines alone
For reasons chilling to the bone
Perhaps more dates would turn out right
If she could curb her appetite

Nauti Buoys

While sailors open drums of rum
To swig below the decks
Indulgent captains who succumb
Are often found in wrecks

Doggone

My dog has died and no one cares
I mention him but this draws stares
And frowns which tell me I'm too old
To mourn a pet, or so I'm told

Empty corners, bare floor
Room before but now we’ve more
Toys donated, bed gone
No more divots in the lawn

Coming home, a rusty gate
Announces me and though I wait
No rocket launches down the path
To knock me down and make me laugh

Quiet mealtimes, no one begs
Or nuzzles gently at my legs
Knowing that, in time, of course I’ll
Slip him the odd, tender morsel

Day is done, I climb the stair
And reach the top but he’s not there
I pray for sleep – those loving scenes
When he runs to me in my dreams

Mind The Gap

Ever go upstairs and not remember why you did?
Or take the groceries out the car but then forget the kid?
Ever open up the fridge and find the teapot in it?
Forget to play the lottery then curse when others win it?

Lose your keys? Kill the grass?
Return home to check the gas?
Fail to find your car though it's right next to where you are
And so you verbally abuse it while more shoppers watch you lose it
Now if you were on the booze it might excuse it...

(let's defuse it)

Scientists would say your frontal lobe is disengaged
You won't remember that, so write this down:

you're middle-aged

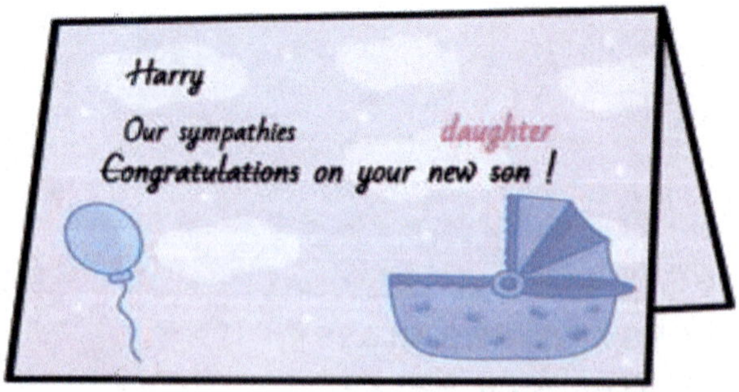

Tudor Suitor

Old King Henry had six wives
Whose days were full of dread
For most of them led tragic lives
Then often wound up dead

Catherine of Aragon
To whom he first proposed
Could not produce a princely son
So he said *Adios!*

Then Anne Boleyn, closer to home
Demanded that they wed
So Henry cut off ties with Rome
But then cut off her head

Poor Jane Seymour was the one
Who finally played her part
When she, at last, produced a son
But died, which broke his heart

Anne of Cleves, the next one booked
Was regal, young and wealthy
The problem was she didn't look
Quite like her royal selfie

Catherine Howard, it was said
No man had ever dated
But rumours spread after they'd wed
So was decapitated

Catherine Parr, a lively sort
Who wielded her own power
Helped organise his kids and court
Once she'd escaped The Tower

All Henry wanted was a son
A prince whom he could teach
To rule his people when he'd gone
But this was out of reach

The irony which overwhelms
This patriarchal scene?
He gave to England and its realms
Perhaps their greatest queen

Because Young Bess, put to the test
Excelled in her employ
And showed the world it takes a girl
To do it like a boy

Hue and Cry

On the news they warn: *The city's now a combat zone*
Turned off the TV and went outside to be alone

Some I know are marching, mostly peaceful, others not
Strangers are now asking me if I'm a patriot

Sitting in my garden, how I love the peace and quiet
I'll fight for a cause but I'm not brave enough to riot

Everyone has history, the grievance lists are long
Who gets to decide whose version's right and whose is wrong?

Our multi-coloured tapestry is starting to unweave
Can we not live together? Were we just being naive?

I come into my garden for the colours and the light
A joy I'd miss if flowers only came in black or white

Mane Attraction

Rapunzel's prince betrothed his love
Her freedom he was wishing her
Alas, he could not climb above!
(she'd used too much conditioner)

2B Or Not 2B

The brains behind the pencil
Made his mark which we commend
But smarter still's his wife
Who stuck a rubber on the end

Bushwhacked

We have a hedge – when I say *we*
I'm merely being neighbourly
Which separates us from next door
We're *Number Two*, they're *Number Four*

The hedge is green and not too tall
And forms a living, breathing wall
Which houses hedgehogs, snails and toads
Who are no match for busy roads

The problem is, our neighbour's plans
Involve a wall where our hedge stands
Three times its height and twice as thick
He's done all the arithmetic

Just think how private it will be!
I won't see you, you won't see me!
To me, this sentiment offends
Because I'd thought of us as friends

His plan to rip the whole hedge out
This 'eyesore' he could do without
We thought he had it all in hand
Until we learned it's on *our* land

So now he doesn't speak to me
Which happens when folks disagree
Their house put quickly up for sale
A sorry ending to this tale

As for our hedge, it's still intact
And here's an interesting fact:
He'll get his wish without a wall
For soon we won't see him at all

Less Cargo

Our friend, the snail, needs never pack
For all it owns is on its back
It heads out on the open road
Quite unencumbered by its load

You won't find snails in top hotels
Instead they curl up in their shells
Emerging when they feel the need
To partake in their evening feed

We mock the snail, its sluggish pace
And yet some pay to watch them race
Ironic, say the French, and crude
Who view them solely as fast food

Sole Mates

Park Guy
Running by
Catching everybody's eye
Chiseled face
Killer pace
Never comes in second place
Hasn't time to stop and chat
Training isn't meant for that
Sprints past like a thoroughbred
Focused on the road ahead
You enflame
It's a game
Will I ever learn your name?
Park Guy
Running by
Catching everybody's eye

Watch Your Tongue

When canny cannibals suggest
You call 'round as a dinner guest
You're right to feel suspicious
They're hoping you're delicious

And if the book next to the pan
Is *How To Serve Your Fellow Man*
It's time to quit the venue
'Cause guess who's on the menu?

Beached Wail

The Great White's famous for its size
So when you see its dorsal
It shouldn't come as a surprise
You may be its next morsel
Don't try to swim or duck and dive
From *Carcharodon carcharias*
It views each move to stay alive
As utterly hilarious
But be aware some do swim by
For quite another reason
Just hope you never catch its eye
During the mating season

Game of Cones

I have a dog whose name is Spark
Who often takes me to the park
Where we enjoy an evening stroll
I feed the ducks, he's on patrol

An old pro, he knows all the tricks
From playing dead to fetching sticks
His latest one involves a scheme
Which bags him loads of free ice cream

He'll spy a toddler on his own
Who's struggling with a waffle cone
One far too big for little hands
And all the balance that demands

Spark uses charm and big, brown eyes
To get him closer to the prize
Then as he nears the little ones
That's when he grabs the cone and runs

I'm deeply saddened by each theft
And every howl from the bereft
Whose double-scoops of lemon lime
Perpetuate his life of crime

The mothers round on Spark and curse
And I make sure they're reimbursed
Which throws the whole plan in reverse
For he was taught to steal a purse

Branch Locator

Without any apology
I traced my genealogy
In hope I'd find an entry
Replete with well-heeled gentry

Perhaps a Duke without an heir
Yet to bequeath his titled lair
Or better yet a Duchess
Who'd keep me in her clutches

I dreamed of billionaire tycoons
Who sipped and supped from silver spoons
Whose present state of wealth
Fared better than their health

But no! I learned my great-great-gran
Was jailed because she shot a man
Who wooed her in a heath
Then ran off with her teeth

Another ancestor trained bears
To ride on bikes and dance on chairs
Until they grew to hate him
I guess that's why they ate him

Much further back, one of our crowd
Could summon rain down from a cloud
But locals weren't that smitten
Because they lived in Britain

If you've swung through my family tree
Please have the cheque made out to me
Because this brachiator
Wants paying now, not later

A Sine of Genus

Imagine sitting by a lake
And wondering what it would take
To calculate its area
The formula would scare ya

Or fancy while beneath a tree
You're struck by thoughts of gravity
Quite tough with which to grapple
Whilst munching on an apple

Or say you're watching tortoises
When what you start to notice is
Through lack of adaptation
They face annihilation

Imagine peering into space
Amazed how it all hangs in place
Then arguing dark matter
Might make the cosmos scatter

Great minds considered these and more
From ancient Greece to Ecuador
This group of geeks is quite well-versed
At sorting out our universe

What theorem might I devise?
Am I not wise? There is some doubt
For I've just only realised
You close the fridge... the light goes out

Secret Santa

The day before The Night Before
The office turned into a store
With gifts galore from Santa's stock
At lunchtime, right on one o'clock

A furtive glance across the room
Saw someone wrapping a perfume
While camouflaged behind a fern
(the new girl had lot to learn)

A friend will cough to help a mate
Disguise the sound of sticky tape

Shirley's eyes revealed a glint
Each time she dropped another hint
In knowing just what not to tell
She kept the weak under her spell

And Andy, bless him, the poor dear
Just hoped he'd get it right this year
For Sue, who longed for something French
He'd bought a Jean-Paul Gautier wrench

Old Trevor thought it all a con
A blasphemous phenomenon
Which led to several allegations
His gifts came from petrol stations

All dreams of wintry escapades
Were dashed by half-price wiper blades

Still, pity those who drew Prue's name
The dowager who ran the game
Who claimed its true meaning had gone
Then priced her gift on Amazon

Big Tony came to stuff his face
So ate at an alarming pace
Before they wrapped it up for Luke
Whose wife was just as bad a cook

Stollen, edam, Toblerone
Belgian nougat in a cone
Baby Jesus, Heaven sent
Now came via the continent

I've seen several scars happen
Over a slice of marzipan

Each festive tummy satisfied
The cups and plates all put aside
Fiona rose to give a toast
But belched up Captain Morgan's ghost

Big Lenny then began to sift
And lift until he found his gift:
100ml of CK One
Would do quite nicely for his son

Ooh, it's lovely... that's so sweet!
As girls are wont to coo and tweet
With every present they unwrap
And gaze upon whilst in their lap

Which makes guys pause and think a bit:
This Santa thing's made me a hit
That perfume seemed to animate her
I'll say 'hi' by the laminator

So Merry Christmas one and all
Be pleased you got a gift at all
Enjoy that sip of Triple Sec
In your new purple turtle neck!

Much Ado

If you're flat broke it's said you've got
A fair amount of diddly-squat
And maybe more because this means
You also own a hill of beans
Which may forestall the need to beg
When added to your great goose egg
Combined with zero, zip and zilch
With all of this why would one filch?
Because if you give it more thought
When you've got nought, there's lots you got

Alpha Mail

The moment I turn down your street
There's no one that I wish to meet
So step aside or feel my wrath
'Cause I'm a walking psychopath

I don't care how you feel today
If so-and-so has moved away
Or that you think stamps cost too much
For those who like to stay in touch

I'll kick your pots and slam your gate
And feed that dog of yours I hate
A Reese's Peanut Butter Cup
To make the ugly mutt shut up

As for your kid, if he's on hand
And asks me for a rubber band
He'll get one right between the eyes
Then several more until he cries

And what's the deal with Amazon?
Do you just click 'til it's all gone?
Is it too much to take a bus
And shop just like the rest of us?

Now listen up: if you complain
You won't hear from your gran again
When we hear something we don't like
My friends and me, we go on strike

That's right, we're not like most men
'Cause I'm your local postman

Time Lapse

I brush your hair and talk of things
You still remember
The torch that lit the songs we'd sing
Now just an ember
I pour the tea
You study me
And wonder why
I still come by

I dig out photos of the boys
More reminiscing
Now in a house devoid of noise
Each night you listen
A vigil kept
While fear has crept
Into a mind
That's been confined

Sinatra's on the radio
And works his magic
This world which you no longer know
At once, less tragic

It was our song
You hum along

Then understand
And take my hand

Arch Nemesis

Beware the Ides! foretells the fall
Of he who rose to conquer Gaul
And lands still further from his home
This warrior, this son of Rome

On his return to claim his right
A haruspex with second sight
Met Caesar by the Senate arch
To warn him of the Ides of March

They'd killed an ox and found no spleen
An omen that could only mean
The Consul should fear for his life
As did, Calpurnia, his wife

But Caesar didn't fear the gods
For he had overcome the odds
To overshadow mortal men
And take his seat in Rome again

So came the day, but nothing passed
Until the Senators amassed
Fulfilling what was prophesied
Thus, on the fifteenth, Caesar died

Of every haruspex, it's said
They earn their living from the dead
And though they claim the role of *seer*
It's often what we overhear

Double Cross

But somewhere, somehow Judas turned
And walked away from all he'd learned
So when the two men dipped their bread
They both knew one would soon be dead

We're not sure how it came to this
Why he betrayed him with a kiss
To bring about the earthly end
Of someone he had called a friend

Arrested, tortured, hung to die
As soldiers laughed and women cried
His friend collected his reward
And hoped the cause had been restored

But this betrayal had a price
Which cost poor Judas paradise
He lost his friends then lost all hope
And wound up swinging from a rope

Where is he now? God only knows
Good people pray for his repose
In hope our own friends keep us close
Especially when we need them most

You Can't Be Sirius

The push is on to get to Mars
Because down here we've blown it
I'm just not sure if Mars is ours
For who's to say we own it?

Maybe its own inhabitants
Will greet us when we cruise in
In tiny, shiny disco pants
And shout *We're all called Susan!*

We'll tell them all about the Earth
Its sky, its seas, the land
How right from birth we know the worth
Of taking someone's hand

Of running jumps into a lake
To beat the summer heat
And hopes that Grandma's gonna bake
Our favourite thing to eat

The satisfaction we derive
From finding the right gift
And pulling over when we drive
To give a friend a lift

Why monkeys make us laugh out loud
While spiders make us shriek
How lovers can tune out a crowd
When dancing cheek to cheek

Of course, they'll think us all absurd
Forsaking paradise
But why come here? Haven't you heard?
We've only rocks and ice!

Dumbfounded we would roam so far
They'll note down in their book:
Good Lord, these Earthlings really are as stupid as they look!

Bottom's Up!

Flamingos dine while upside down
Which sometimes makes me think:
How is it that they never drown
Each time they take a drink?

Ready To Chuck It All In

Today the Queen turned ninety-four
Her subjects wish her many more
Except the heir, on bended knee
Who hoped she'd go at ninety-three

Beeline

The honey bee performs a dance
Which indicates the vector
Its friends should fly to find those plants
Providing the best nectar

With six legs that's no easy feat
And so, to overcome it
To keep the message short and sweet
The less adroit just hum it

Ginger Bred

A young prince chose to jet abroad
And start his life anew
Her Majesty had thought it odd
He'd given not a clue

While chess has always been about
The move that's unforeseen
No pawn has ever taken out
A well-defended queen

Captain's Log

Sir Francis Drake had what it takes
To sail around the world
And followed in Magellan's wake
With England's flag unfurled

Along his route he plundered loot
Until the hold was packed
With millions from Brazilians
And the Spaniards he attacked

On his return, the English yearned
To learn of far-off places
Of queens and perils unforeseen
And men with painted faces

Bess knighted Francis on his ship
While desperately hoping
He'd share his tips for crispy chips
And how to blow a smoke ring

Soon after he was off again
And set sail heading west
But Fortune soon abandoned him
In this, his final quest

Sir Francis survived cannon balls
And arrows tipped with poison
But in the end, when Nature called
It ravaged, then destroyed him

For dysentery killed our man
Which almost led to shipwreck
That's why they sealed him in a can
And christened it the poop deck

Seasoned Greetings

When greeting guests in Tokyo
The custom is to bow down low

While in Tibet both old and young
Say *hi* by sticking out their tongue

In France it's chic to peck the cheek
And friends will clap in Mozambique

Though Greenlanders will sniff your face
Before they help you with your case

Most Eskimos rub nose to nose
In India they'll touch your toes

And Zambians will squeeze the thumbs
Of visitors considered chums

Through handshakes, winks and nods we say
I'm pleased that you dropped by today!

And bless those friends who always know
The sign for when it's time to go

Tongue Twister

The rule for fractions when you're young?
It's two-thirds' brains
And one-third tongue

Prickly Heat

My love is like a red, red rose…
One Scottish bard chose to expose
My ex was like a yucca plant
And on the *yeuch,* I'm adamant

Present Tense

The day I want to bake some bread
You'll be the first to know
Were you confused that time I said
I need to make more dough?

And should I wish to buy a goat
Around the holidays
Feel free to name it but take note
I'd like it honey-glazed

A scented candle lets me know
Exactly what you think
You're hoping seated in its glow
At last, my house won't stink

That weird liqueur with toads inside
Distilled by monks in France
Soon made me wish that I had died
Then made me poop my pants

The Cookie Monster sweater seemed
To spread more disarray
On seeing it, the baby screamed
And both cats ran away.

Gym memberships address excess
With workouts on a mat
Do you think I need to de-stress
Or is it that I'm fat?

It's not the gift, John, it's the thought
While this, no doubt, is right
It's what they've thought, not what they've bought
Which keeps me up at night

Constellation Prize

The figure on the mountain knew
Far higher than the eagle flew
Beyond the sun and past the light
Were men who crossed the sky by night

Soon after dusk their fires appeared
Then slowly, once a course was steered
Their caravan set out en masse
To make its empyreal pass

Like beasts migrating on the plains
Like swarms that form to greet the rains
He found no word for the amount
Of travellers he sought to count

A gallery would pass him by
Whose outlines seemed to signify
Proud emblems of a noble clan
Led by an even a greater man

The bearing, always east to west
Suggested they were on a quest
Or maybe searching for a door
They'd passed through in a time before
And so each night he danced and prayed
Around the fire he had made
In hope his kin might see its glow
Then show him all he wished to know

So, with the last beat from his breast
Great Spirit granted this request
And drew his outline in the sky
That men as he should never die

The pessimist with half a glass
Sees no point being gleeful
While optimists will always ask
If theirs comes with a refill

J. Ormsby

About The Author

John Ormsby grew up in Canada where he was fond of storytelling as a boy, although not always for the right reasons, as his parents will attest. Upon graduating from the University of Toronto, he first worked as a copy editor before moving to the UK where he wound up teaching high school.

In his spare time Mr Ormsby enjoys hiding in trees, pretending he owns a tuba and telling strangers they might be related.

To learn more you can visit: mrormsbyatlarge.com

About the Illustrator

Andrea Benko was born in 1990 and received her degree in Electrical Engineering in 2011. She worked for a nearly a decade within the field before discovering her passion for drawing which led to a change of career as an illustrator. Her signature style uses simple lines, humorous characters and vivid colours to bring words to life.

In her spare time Ms Benko enjoys chess, going for walks, reading and doodling just for the heck of it.

For more information about Ms Benko's artwork, please check out:

https://andreabenko.art.blog/

Printed in Great Britain
by Amazon

34921039R00046